Copyright © Rev. Dr. S. D'Montford. Monday, Octob

Shambhallah Awareness Centre brings you: -

"THE CANCER ANSWER"
AND AUSTRALAIN STORY
BY DR. SHÉ D'MONTFORD
ISBN: 978-0-9757535-7-6

Written By Rev. Dr. S. D'Montford - Cover Artwork by © Copyright Rev, Dr, S. D'Montford, Friday, October 25, 2010 Gold Coast Australia. Published by Shambhallah Awareness Centre for educational purposes. **All Rights Reserved.** The information presented is protected under the Berne Convention for the Protection of Literature and Artistic works, under other international conventions and under national laws on copyright and neighbouring rights. Extracts of the information in this book may be reviewed, but not reproduce without express written permission from the publisher. Reproduction or translation of portions of this publication requires explicit, prior authorisation in writing. **Disclaimer:** The primary reason for this publication is entertainment and education about Pagan practices. While Shambhallah Awareness Centre has used all reasonable endeavours to ensure the information in this book is as accurate as possible, it gives no warranty or guarantee that the material, information, or publications made accessible by them are fit for any use whatsoever nor does that excuse you from using your common-sense. Shambhallah Awareness Centre and Rev. Dr S. D'Montford accepts no liability or responsibility for any loss or damage whatsoever suffered as a result of direct or indirect use or application of any material, publication or information obtained from them.

Shambhallah Awareness Centre is a tax exempt Pagan Church and a not for profit organisation
P.O. Box 3541, Helensvale Town Centre. Q. 4212
http://www.shambhallah.org

Special Thanks to:-
Ken Wills, Geoff Everitt, Duncan Roads

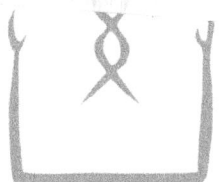

CONTENTS:

THE CANCER ANSWER	ON PAGE 4
WHAT IS LAETRILE?	ON PAGE 6
HYDROGEN CYANIDE & ENZYMES	ON PAGE 7
FALSE TESTING & VESTED INTERESTS	ON PAGE 9
WHY WOULD THIS BE ALLOWED TO HAPPEN?	ON PAGE 11
A PERSONAL HISTORY	ON PAGE 13
PERMITS FOR LAETRILE	ON PAGE 18
TAKING PERSONAL RESPONSIBILITY FOR YOUR OWN HEALTH	ON PAGE 25
REFERENCES	ON PAGE 26
CHEMO ONLY 2% EFFECTIVE	ON PAGE 26
CANCER & LAETRILE QUOTES	ON PAGE 27
ABOUT THE AUTHOR	ON PAGE 42

Copyright © Rev. Dr. S. D'Montford. Monday, October 25, 2010 Mackay Qld. Australia.

The Cancer Answer

Laetrile, B-17, Amygdalin & Cancer - An Australian Story.

By Rev Dr S. D'Montford

Has the knowledge of the success of alternative cancer treatments utilising amygdalin, vitamin B17 or Laetrile, been denied by the medical/ pharmaceutical establishment and governmental authorities because it threatens the stranglehold of "the cancer industry" over our own health care choices?

Copyright © Rev. Dr. S. D'Montford. Monday, October 25, 2010 Mackay Qld. Australia.

THE CANCER ANSWER

This article is not intended to give medical advice. I am not a medical doctor. The intention of this article is to raise questions as to the vested interests of research results and testing methods. It is also a retelling of a personal account that should raise ethical concerns, which demand answers. This article only reports and retells facts, research and statements from others who have been involved in cancer research. The purpose of this article is not to claim a cure for cancer rather it is an act of responsible freedom of speech that should raise questions that need addressing about the study of treatments for cancer.

My father was the first person to introduce laetrile into Australia 35-years-ago. After my father did this, people suffering from various forms of cancer chose to use it to successfully treat themselves. However, testing was refused despite its apparent amazing results in thousands of cases, with many willing to give written accounts of their personal experiences. Since 1963 there have been over 100,000 cancer patients treated successfully with laetrile and other alternative methods at the Contreras Hospital in Mexico alone. (http://www.oasisofhope.com) The late Dr. Ernesto Contreras Sr. was a vocal supporter of laetrile treatment. This hospital is his legacy.

I too have been handed a legacy. As a 12-year-old, I witnessed individuals identifying themselves as being from 'Therapeutic Goods,' approach my father with threats of financial ruin to try to dissuade him from importing and distributing this substance before any Australian legislation had been passed against it. More on this later. When laetrile was finally officially tested in Queensland in 2003 it was shown to be effective. See the Queensland Health Circular 02/2003 stating this, reproduced here for your convenience. Despite being tested and approved eight years ago, sufferers are still not being made aware of laetrile as a possible effective alternative, thereby curtailing

Copyright © Rev. Dr. S. D'Montford. Monday, October 25, 2010 Mackay Qld. Australia.

their ability to make informed choices for their own health care. This is a far from acceptable situation.

Policy	DRUGS AND POISONS: Approvals - Queensland Health Policy on the Issue of Approvals for Amygdalin (Vitamin B17 /Laetrile) Under the *Health (Drugs and Poisons Regulation 1996*

Enquiries to:	Drugs and Poisons Services Environmental Health Unit
Telephone:	(07) 3234 0938
Facsimile:	(07) 3234 1480
Our Ref:	A10030572

OFFICE OF THE DIRECTOR-GENERAL

CIRCULAR NO. 02/2003

QUEENSLAND HEALTH POLICY ON THE ISSUE OF APPROVALS FOR AMYGDALIN
(VITAMIN B17/LAETRILE) UNDER THE
HEALTH (DRUGS AND POISONS) REGULATION 1996

Background

Amygdalin is listed in Appendix C of the Standard for the Uniform Scheduling of Drugs and Poisons (the Standard). Substances listed in Appendix C of the Standard are those poisons that are considered of such danger to health as to warrant prohibition of sale, supply and use. Accordingly, all Appendix C poisons of the Standard are regulated poisons under Queensland's *Health (Drugs and Poisons) Regulation 1996* and specific approval is required for them to be obtained, possessed and used.

The Commonwealth Therapeutic Goods Administration (TGA) controls the Special Access Scheme. Category A of this scheme is for use by doctors in the treatment of patients with a life-threatening illness. This scheme is a notification scheme only. The scheme provides for access to normally inaccessible drugs where the doctor certifies the drug is necessary for a life threatening illness in the particular patient. The TGA is also responsible for regulating which substances are allowed to be imported into Australia. Amygdalin is contained in Schedule 8 to the *Customs (Prohibited Imports) Regulations 1956*. Therefore, for any Amygdalin that needs to be sourced from overseas, an import permit is issued by the TGA following their receipt of a Category A notification form by a treating doctor.

Whilst the TGA issues these import permits, this does not allow the treating doctor or the patient to be in possession of or to use Amygdalin under Queensland Health legislation. Specific approval is still required from Queensland Health for this purpose.

Office	Postal	Phone	Fax
19th floor	GPO Box 48	(07) 3234 1170	(07) 3234 1482
Queensland Health Building	BRISBANE QLD 4001		
147 - 163 Charlotte Street			
BRISBANE QLD 4000			

Before I proceed with telling my father's story in more detail, I should explain what laetrile is and why it works.

WHAT IS LAETRILE?

Laetrile is the name of vitamin B17, also known as Amygdaline. Vitamin B17 occurs naturally in many foods including strawberries, cashews, cassava, apple seeds, peach and apricot kernels. Laetrile can be consumed harmlessly from these sources. Many alternative practitioners claim that regular consumption of B17 can keep cancer at bay and is an effective treatment for many organ and skin cancers. Forms of this substance have been used in the treatment of human cancer in western medicine from 1843. Traditional Chinese medicine has used peach kernels, also known as bitter almonds, that contain significant quantities of laetrile in the treatment of tumours for 3,000 years. Its effectiveness was so legendary that peaches are associated with immortality in Chinese culture. Zhang Guo Lao, one of the Eight Chinese Immortals, associated with health and healing, is depicted carrying a Peach of Immortality. Yet, administrative bodies began actively opposing laetrile treatments as 'potentially toxic' in the 1970's and heavily promoted undeniably toxic chemotherapy in its place, even though some studies show chemotherapy to be less than 2% effective. (Morgan G et al. *The Contribution of Cytotoxic Chemotherapy to 5-year Survival in Adult Malignancies.* Clinical Oncology (2004); 16:549-560 - Barton MB et al. *Radiation Therapy: Are We Getting Value For Money?* Clin Oncol (R Coll Radiol) 1996;8(3):206)

Those who say that vitamin B17 is not a cure for cancer are technically correct. It is only the human body that cures cancer. In the same way it is the human body not the taking of supplements of vitamin B1, which are given by injection or taken by mouth, that cures beriberi. Yet, the human body cannot cure itself of beriberi without supplements of vitamin B1. As I understand it, cancer cells are omnipresent in the human body, and are only life-threatening when these get out of control. Laetrile appears to be the switch to control these cells and keep them friendly. Deficiency in B17 may be a significant contributing factor to cancer cells becoming aggressive. The more we understand B17, the more it makes cancer look like it is a nutritional deficiency disease. We accept and understand other nutritional deficiency diseases like scurvy, which can occur if we stop consuming foods with vitamin C. Pellagra can occur if we do not consume foods containing enough vitamin B. Cancer is increasingly appearing to occur if we do not consume foods that are rich in nitrilosides/vitamin B17.

HYDROGEN CYANIDE AND ENZYMES

The studies of Ernst T. Krebs, Jr., Dr. Sc. from as early as 1952, and many others through to the present, who have duplicated his findings, show that vitamin B17 is in the cyanide family but it is good cyanide. It is two parts glucose, one part hydrogen cyanide and one part benzaldehyde (an analgesic). Hydrogen cyanide is non-toxic when taken as a food or in controlled doses as a refined pharmaceutical. Commonly consumed substances such as salt and sugar can be up to twenty times more toxic. Krebs claimed that the body breaks down B17 using the enzyme rhodanese, which changes it into thiocyanate and benzoic acid. These are beneficial, working with B12 to nourish the body. Excesses of these by-products are expelled from the body via urine. Krebs' works demonstrated that rhodanese has an inverse relationship to cancer cells, it is found everywhere in a normal healthy body, but not where cancer cells exist. However, the enzyme beta-glucosidase has a direct relationship to cancer cells and is found in very large quantities around them. If there is no cancer in the body there is no enzyme beta-glucosidase. However, when B17 comes into contact with beta-glucosidase that is present in large quantities around colonies of cancer cells, a chemical reaction occurs and the hydrogen cyanide and benzaldehyde combine and produce a poison, which destroys only cancer cells. This process is known as selective toxicity. See diagram.

Diagram Credit: Copyright © Rev. Dr. S. D'Montford.

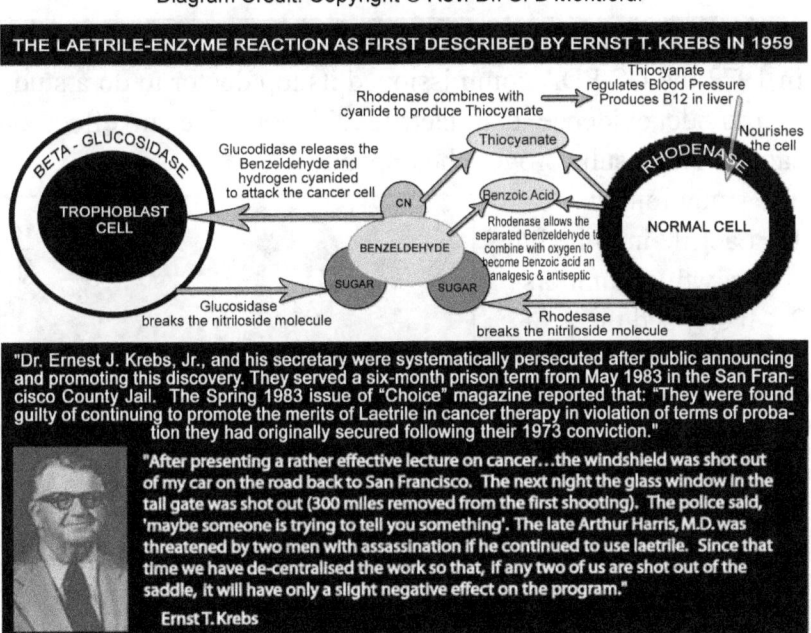

Why does one substance, laetrile, appear to be selectively toxic against most cancers when there are hundreds of different kinds? Though Ernst T. Krebs, had only an honorary doctorate, he found that the only constant, the malignant or neoplastic component in all exhibitions of cancer, is susceptible to the laetrile reaction's specific toxicity. This is the trophoblast. Trophoblast cells are primitive cells that have a fierce antithesis to all other cell types including their somatic or hostal cells. As he said: *"Cancer is trophoblast in spatial and temporal anomaly, hybridised with and vascularized by hostal or somatic cells and in irreversible and fiercely malignant antithesis to such."* Therefore we are looking at any specialist cell that mutates into a typical less evolved and more aggressive form. B17 is therefore a typical treatment for a typical cell type.

FALSE TESTING & VESTED INTERESTS

In 1972 the US FDA commissioned its top doctor to do a study to provide evidence that laetrile did not have an effect on cancer. The results proved the opposite.

The study found:
1. Laetrile inhibited the growth of tumours
2. It stopped the spreading (metastasising) of cancer in mice
3. It relieved pain
4. It acted as a cancer preventative
5. It improved general health

Dr Sugiura & Ralph Moss

Dr Kanematsu Sugiura was the senior laboratory researcher at the Sloan Ketting Cancer Institute. He reported in his experiments with mice that Laetrile was more effective in the control of cancer than any substance he had ever tested. This was not acceptable to his superiors. Instead of being pleased at the possibility of a breakthrough, they brought in other researchers to duplicate Sugiura's experiments to try to prove that they were faulty. Instead the follow-up studies confirmed

> 11/24/77 New York Times
>
> ## Cancer Aide Out in Laetrile Dispute
>
> **By SHEILA RULE**
>
> The assistant public affairs director of the Memorial Sloan-Kettering Cancer Center has been discharged because he helped write a report charging that the center's research into the controversial cancer drug laetrile was incomplete and scientifically invalid.
>
> The assistant director, Ralph W. Moss, was discharged Monday after he told another center official he was the co-author of the report for a group called Second Opinion, which consists of staff members of Sloan-Kettering who investigate problems at the institution. At a news conference last Friday, Mr. Moss appeared on behalf of the group and released the report, which alleges that a negative report on laetrile released by the center last June omitted some experiments that indicated the drug might be effective in treating cancer.
>
> Second Opinion is not sanctioned by Sloan-Kettering. Mr. Moss is the only member of the center who has publicly linked himself to the group and the only member discharged.
>
> "There also were major errors in the way some experiments were performed by Sloan-Kettering, Mr. Moss said yesterday of the cancer research institution at 1275 York Avenue, at 68th Street, in Manhattan. "We are not pro-laetrile but we feel this is a matter for scientific debate. There has been a cover-up."
>
> Jerry Delaney, director of public affairs at the center, said Mr. Moss was discharged because he "betrayed the trust placed in him as a member of the public affairs department of this cancer center."
>
> "By declaring himself an author and spokesman for the group," Mr. Delaney continued, "which stands in outspoken opposition to the most fundamental principles and policies of this cancer center, he has acted in a manner that conflicts with his most basic job responsibilities."
>
> Mr. Delaney said Second Opinion's charges were "absurd," and that the group had a reputation of "issuing papers and statements that we feel are irresponsible and totally incorrect."
>
> Mr. Moss said he was asked by Mr. Delaney last Thursday to ttend the news conference with a tape recorder to report on Second Opinion. At that time, the center knew nothing of his activities with the group, Mr. Moss said.
>
> Mr. Moss refused to represent the center at the news conference "because of conscience" but told Mr. Delaney he would take the day off and attend as an observer. Mr. Delaney said he would represent Sloan-Kettering.

Sugiura.

Undaunted, his superiors called for new experiments, following procedures which where designed to make the tests fail. Eventually they did, and it was only that failure that was announced to the world. Dr. Ralph Moss was The Assistant Director of Public Affairs at Sloan-Kettering at the time of the Laetrile tests.

When he was ordered by his superiors to release false information about the results of those tests, he resigned this position in protest. Dr. Ralph Moss later wrote a book on this scandalous situation called, "The Cancer Industry," in which he protested against this cover-up and was subsequently fired in November 1977 for *"failing to carry out my most basic job responsibility, which means to lie when your boss tells you to"*. However, this book hardly raised an eyebrow in the medical world.

WHY WOULD THIS BE ALLOWED TO HAPPEN?

To make sense of something that seems bureaucratic and nonsensical, follow the money. The money says this: When a person is diagnosed as having cancer, as many as seven people are directly employed in their treatment. With hundreds of thousands of people being diagnosed with cancer each year this ensures seven times as many jobs are secured. It should also be remembered that billions of dollars are poured into the fundraising process for cancer research, which is itself a huge industry employing thousands. A small percentage of those funds raised are not used up in the process of fundraising. The remaining funds filter through to a self-perpetuating research process. If a cure were declared, what would happen to the jobs of all of these people? It does not appear to be in the best interest of these people to declare that a very effective treatment has been tested and found.

How, under these circumstances, is it possible to remove a vested interest in NOT finding a cure, from this huge, convoluted, bureaucratic process?

Add to this that the drug companies have stockpiles of current treatments that are very toxic, limited in their results, and are fetching very good prices. This means that it would not be a sensible option to declare an easy, cheap, non-toxic and readily available solution that requires little or no specialist training in its administration, to be obtainable on the market any time soon. It could be seen as being a thing that could be contrary to certain vested interests or justified as 'not good for the stockholders.' This untenable situation could be defended on the grounds of economic rationalisation. i.e. 'Let a few of them die for the greater good.' Yet the reality is that just like the Morlock and the Eloi, in H. G. Wells' "The Time Machine," one part of society is surviving on the suffering and death of the other.

It was for this and other reasons that two times Nobel Prize winner, Linus Pauling PhD (1901-1994) claimed that; *"Everyone should know that most cancer research is largely a fraud..."*
"Cancer Conspirsy" -1989- ©LP Recordings P/L Sydney & http://www.brainyquote.com/quotes/authors/l/linus_pauling.html

Some might try to excuse the authorities as not knowing these facts. However Hans Nieper M.D. a world famous oncologist who uses laetrile made this statement: *"You wouldn't believe how many FDA officials or relatives or acquaintances of FDA officials come to see me as patients in Hanover. You wouldn't believe this, or directors of the AMA, or ACA, or the presidents of orthodox cancer institutes. That's the fact."*

Many might be shocked by these statements and believe that a serious, fraudulent, mass-life-threatening situation could never happen in modern times, yet I was an eye-witness to open statements that such shocking economic rationalisation is a driving force behind the cancer industry.

A PERSONAL HISTORY

This story begins some 35-years-ago when my father, Geoffery Everitt, was the first person to import Laetrile into Australia. Dad had a new health foods company "Vitalife" and was the first person in the world to flavour mineral water called "Goldspa." The only other Australian vitamin company at the time was "Blackmores." The market was wide open and my father had positioned himself well. At the time laetrile was not prohibited so it seemed like a good investment to add to his stable, but my father soon became aware of the overwhelming human need behind it. It was more than a mere product. Dad could see that it was really helping people. However, my father was soon to realise that he was an idealistic man in a far from idealistic world.

Dad ran the business from home. Our large double garage had become our stock room. He had two drivers and was responsible for his own distribution. It was common for people to come to the home in order to conduct business with Dad. He would often do business deals standing in the garage, sweaty from lugging boxes of stock. I was only 12-years-old yet I clearly remember some men in black suits with posh accents arguing with my father in the front yard of our house. I went outside to investigate the commotion. Dad was finishing a very intense and in depth conversation with these men in black. They looked at each other and rolled their eyes. I clearly remember hearing them say, "Mr Everitt, you don't understand, we simply cannot allow you to import something that might *damage the cancer industry* if people begin self-prescribing." My father rarely raised his voice or got upset, yet he swore at these men, told me to go inside and told them to leave. As I was going inside I heard one of the men say to my father that if he refused to co-operate they would ruin him and all of his businesses.

"Who was that?" I asked my father when he came inside.
"Representatives from Therapeutic Goods" he replied.
"What do they mean by *The Cancer Industry*."" I queried.
"Cancer appears to be making a lot of people a lot of money," he stated. "Whenever obviously stupid decisions are made by men in power, the reason can be found by following the money."

I was so angry. I understood what they had meant before my father explained it, I just couldn't believe it. These were people who were supposed to be altruistically looking out for our best interests, however, they revealed on our front lawn, that they were serving the best interests of big business. It had vague déja vu realism. At twelve, it was like someone telling me that my worst nightmares were real, that the bogyman was real, he was out to get everyone and he made money out of letting people die. I don't think this anger has ever left me; it only grew as I observed what happened to my father, a truly altruistic man trying to help others.

Within a few weeks, these men in black began to make good on their threats. Legislation was swiftly passed that saw laetrile busted down to a 'Pet Food Only' licence. Yet people still bought it. When it became obvious that the health food stores were happy to keep stocking it in the pet section, Dad found that his service station licences were not renewed and that he was unable to buy bottles for his mineral water. Apparently there had been mass purchases by a subsidiary of Coca Cola, which, I believe, is in itself, a subsidiary of Monsanto, one of the largest drug companies in the world. Being the first person in the world to flavour mineral water should have made Dad a millionaire several times over, yet his ethics prevented him selling out. Dad had to let this part of his business fall by the wayside. Somehow Dad kept going. He kept suppling and distributing laetrile. The demand for the product was overwhelming. The testimonies were flooding in for this much needed substance. These testimonies where disregarded by the authorities as merely anecdotal evidence and not real case studies.

A single story was circulated in the press that a man had obtained B17 from a veterinarian; In those days B17 was used by vets in the treatment of heartworm in animals. This article claimed that the man had injected himself with a massive dose of B17, resulting in his own death. We tried to find out who this man was and to gain further details of his death, but we were blocked at every turn. We could not even locate a single person who knew him personally. However, several people came forward, including one vet, claiming that the circulated story must be false. They claimed to have injected themselves with extremely large doses of laetrile in an attempt to prove that it was not toxic. The only side effects reported by these people were heart palpitations in some and excessive sleep for others. Understanding the chemical processes involved, it seems unlikely that a large injection of veterinary grade laetrile would have been able to cause a person's death, as the body's enzymes naturally breaks it into non-toxic substances that specifically target cancer or are excreted. These claims were also refuted without testing. So by the end of the year, B17 was completely banned. Yet banning a product does not stop people who have used it and have had successful results with it, from trying to procure it. People were turning up on our doorstep at all hours of the day and night, from as far away as Tasmania and New Zealand, begging for any stocks we might have left. It was heart wrenching.

My father lost heart, and lost the will to fight. He decided it was best to look after his own family. He dropped it all - Bought another service station for a while and finally retied early as a carer for his wife and their only natural child, my step-brother, until they both died. Dad lives happily now and remarried the love of his life at 72-years of age. He is as fit as a mally bull. Healthier than most men in their fifties.

However, Dad tried to appeal the ban and have B17 scientifically and clinically tested so that Therapeutic Goods would have no other choice but to approve it. Testing was refused on the grounds that they did not have the funding to proceed with the tests. Ironically, billions of dollars are thrown at 'the cancer industry' every year, yet they could not find the resources to investigate the successful results that people had achieved by using B17. In fact it is curious that with all of the money and time that has been given to cancer research, no solutions have been forth coming. But why would they kill the golden goose by finding answers? Shouldn't we be demanding to know WHY after all of this time, these researchers still can't even tell us the most basic things about cancer like how and why cancer begins? Yet, as shown here, Krebs' theory behind why laetrile works, purports that an answer to this question has been known since 1950, and additionally, a cancer answer.

When there is a large vested interest in the way, potentially preventing people getting the best medical care possible, we must not allow ourselves to be terrified into believing that the only option is 'their' less than satisfactory option. We must educate ourselves and demand the right to self-determination of our health until those with a vested interest are not able to prevent access to the solutions they supposedly seek on our behalf.

Angel Rodriguez of http://www.b17.com.au concludes, *"Cancer is BIG business! The Cancer Drug companies have made every effort and attempt to make it illegal and unavailable through their lobbying of the governments and through their financial influence on the large charitable cancer institutions. Its all about $$$$ in the Mutli BILLION DOLLAR CANCER INDUSTRY!"*

"...every effort and attempt..." seems to extend to post testing suppression of information. Even though B17 has now been tested and approved for use by Queensland Health over eight years ago, information about its effectiveness is still not being made readily available. We can see why, now we must demand that it be made more readily available. Socrates showed that civil disobedience is a vital part of avoiding despotism in a democratic society. We are making headway on this. WE ARE WINNING – We have moved one small step closer to getting laetrile recognised legally.

PERMITS FOR LAETRILE

Not only has Queensland Health approved laetrile for use through ethical oncologists, now there is also a way for the wider community to be able to legally obtain it by following the formality of applying for a permit issued by the

Therapeutic Goods Association in Canberra. This is one more step in the right direction. See sample attached.

Yet there is a long way to go. We have to send petitions and individually email these departments demanding more right of self-determination in this matter given the many studies that have been done confirming its safety and effectiveness. Here are some other well known doctors, not as yet mentioned in this article, who have published papers and studies favouring laetrile from 1962 to the present: - Dr. John Morrone, Manuel Navarro, M.D., Burton Goldberg, Robert Atkins, M.D., Dr. Emesto Contreras, Dr. Michael Schachter, Dr. Douglas, P.E. Binzel. The body of evidence in favour of laetrile's effectiveness and safety far out ways those against it.
The freeing of draconian control by authority occurs due to fear
The freeing of draconian control by authority occurs due to fear of a growing tide of overwhelming public opinion. Freedoms are restored to prevent revolution occurring. We have to let them know that we are very unhappy with this situation. If enough people demand that B17 be freely available, the ridiculous restrictions will be completely lifted on the use of laetrile from both refined and natural sources. The powers that be will have to finally loosen their strangle hold on 'the cancer industry.'

If you wish to obtain a legal permit you must proceed on this next stage with caution as the following approvals and permits contain ambiguous language, used to protect the departments involved. However, this double speak could be used against the applicant. It is my opinion that you should keep written and sound recorded records of all phone conversations with any government departments in these matters in order to be able to demonstrate open communication, approval and intent, both yours and theirs. Making a copy of all records and storing them in a separate location from the originals is practical, in case one set is lost or goes missing.

Here are the six steps that will enable you to legally purchase laetrile in Australia: -

1. Obtain a "TGA Notification For Category 'A' Permit Request Form" permit from the TGA in Canberra, or you can download a copy of them from: -
2. http://www.b17.com.au/copy.asp?sect=downloads&page=downloads
3. A doctor will need to sign and complete it with you.
4. Then you must contact the 'Special Access Scheme' via phone on 0262328111, to obtain details on the supply of unapproved medicines in Australia. Record the name of the person that you have spoken to and fax them a copy personally.
5. Make sure that you inform them you require a permit to be urgently faxed back to you that day.
6. Call your contact again immediately after you have faxed them the form, to make sure that they have received it and record the time they received it next to their name.

You should receive your permit faxed back within 24-hours. Once you have the permit there are many reputable sources to order laetrile from overseas. Many can be sourced on the Internet. Again a personal contact via a phone call is always a good idea.

Here follows documentation on: -

Copyright © Rev. Dr. S. D'Montford. Monday, October 25, 2010 Mackay Qld. Australia.

- The current rulings, 3 pages
- An application form 1 page and
- One man's personal letter-in-reply from the TGA

Copyright © Rev. Dr. S. D'Montford. Monday, October 25, 2010 Mackay Qld. Australia.

Enquiries to: Drugs & Poisons Policy &
Regulation Unit
Environmental Health Branch
Telephone: (07) 3328 9310
Facsimile: (07) 3328 9354
Our Ref: QV060545

OFFICE OF THE DIRECTOR-GENERAL

CIRCULAR NO. 01/2006

QUEENSLAND HEALTH POLICY ON THE ISSUE OF APPROVALS FOR AMYGDALIN (VITAMIN B17/LAETRILE) UNDER THE HEALTH (DRUGS AND POISONS) REGULATION 1996

This Circular rescinds and replaces Circular 02/2003 of the same title.

Background

Amygdalin is listed in Appendix C of the Standard for the Uniform Scheduling of Drugs and Poisons (the Standard). Substances listed in Appendix C of the Standard are those poisons that are considered of such danger to health as to warrant prohibition of sale, supply and use. Accordingly, all Appendix C poisons of the Standard are regulated poisons under Queensland's *Health (Drugs and Poisons) Regulation 1996* and specific approval is required for them to be obtained, possessed and used.

The Commonwealth Therapeutic Goods Administration (TGA) controls the Special Access Scheme. Category A of this scheme is for use by medical practitioners in the treatment of patients with a life-threatening illness. This scheme is a notification scheme only. The scheme provides for access to normally inaccessible drugs where the medical practitioner certifies the drug is necessary for a life threatening illness in the particular patient. The TGA is also responsible for regulating which substances are allowed to be imported into Australia. Amygdalin is contained in Schedule 8 to the *Customs (Prohibited Imports) Regulations 1956*. Therefore, for any Amygdalin that needs to be sourced from overseas, an import permit is issued by the TGA following their receipt of a Category A notification form by a treating medical practitioner.

Whilst the TGA issues these import permits, this does not allow the treating medical practitioners or the patient to be in possession of or to use Amygdalin under Queensland Health legislation. Specific approval is still required from Queensland Health for this purpose.

Queensland Health approval

Queensland Health has issued a limited number of approvals to medical practitioners to use Amygdalin under strict guidelines in specific patients. This policy document has been developed to provide clear and concise information concerning the circumstances under which Queensland Health will consider issuing an approval to a medical practitioner for the treatment of a patient with

Office
19ᵗʰ Floor
Queensland Health Building
147 - 163 Charlotte Street
BRISBANE QLD 4000

Postal
GPO Box 48
BRISBANE QLD 4001

Phone
(07) 323 41170

Fax
(07) 323 41482

Amygdalin It should be noted that approval applications are considered on a case-by-case basis and that not all previous applications have been approved.
Criteria for obtaining Queensland Health approval

1. Due to relative toxicity concerns, Queensland Health **will not** issue approval for treatment with **oral Amygdalin**, and will only consider applications for intravenous or intramuscular treatment under a strict treatment protocol.
2. Any relevant specialist's/oncologist's reports relating to the patient's medical condition must be included with the application.
3. Approvals will **only** be considered for patients with an advanced malignancy where all possible conventional treatment has been exhausted.
4. The patient who is to be treated with Amygdalin must be informed of the following relating to the facts about Amygdalin and provide written consent to treatment:
   - the process by which the Amygdalin is manufactured may not be subject to quality control;
   - the potential cyanide toxicity associated with Amygdalin; and
   - the lack of scientific evidence relating to the efficacy of Amygdalin.

The form entitled "Drugs and Poisons: Application for Approval to Obtain, Possess and Use Amygdalin - Informed Consent" has been developed to facilitate the provision of such written informed consent. This form is available at the web address www.health.qld.gov.au. A completed and signed (by the patient) informed consent form must be included with the application.

In order for the patient to provide informed consent, the treating medical practitioner must provide and discuss with the patient the two fact sheets compiled by Queensland Health entitled:
   - "Drugs and Poisons Fact Sheet: Amygdalin/Laetrile - Patient Information"; and
   - "Drugs and Poisons Fact Sheet: Amygdalin/Laetrile - Questions and Answers"

These fact sheets are available at the above web address.

Making application for Queensland Health approval

- All applications must be made in writing by the treating medical practitioner. An application form entitled "Drugs and Poisons: Application by a Medical Practitioner for Approval to Obtain, Possess and Use Amygdalin" has been developed to simplify the process for making application for an approval. This form is also available at the above web address.
- The application form must be completed in full and signed by the treating medical practitioner making the application. (If approvals are issued, they are issued to the treating medical practitioner for a specific patient. Queensland Health approvals are not issued to the patient.)
- Applications must include the following attachments:
   - the informed consent form "Drugs and Poisons: Application for Approval to Obtain, Possess and Use Amygdalin - Informed Consent", completed and signed by the patient; and
   - any relevant specialist's/oncologist's reports relating to the patient's medical condition.

Applications can be made by facsimile, provided the original is submitted by mail as soon as practicable after the facsimile.

Applications should be addressed to:
The Chief Executive, Queensland Health
C/- The Principal Environmental Health Officer
Drugs and Poisons Policy and Regulation
Environmental Health Unit
Queensland Health
PO Box 2368
FORTITUDE VALLEY Q 4006.

Copyright © Rev. Dr. S. D'Montford. Monday, October 25, 2010 Mackay Qld. Australia.

Australian Government
Department of Health and Ageing
Therapeutic Goods Administration

CATEGORY A FORM SPECIAL ACCESS SCHEME

READ CAREFULLY BEFORE COMPLETING

This completed document constitutes the legal authority for an Australian sponsor to supply the specified product and should be forwarded to the Australian Sponsor of the product, accompanied by a prescription where necessary.

A copy of the form must be forwarded to the TGA within 28 days of its completion.
Send to: Medical Officer - SAS, TGA, PO BOX 100, WODEN ACT 2606 [Fax No: (02) 6232 8112 for medicines; and (02) 6232 8785 for medical devices]

The basis for these SAS arrangements is that responsibility for prescribing an unapproved therapeutic good appropriately rests with the patient's medical practitioner and the patient. Category A patients are defined in the legislation as "persons who are seriously ill with a condition from which death is reasonably likely to occur within a matter of months, or from which premature death is reasonably likely to occur in the absence of early treatment". Under s31A(2) and 41JD of the *Therapeutic Goods Act 1989* (the Act) the TGA may seek clarification of the Category A classification of patients. In addition, under s61(3A) of the Act the TGA may release details of inappropriate supply and/or use of unapproved medicines and medical devices to State and Territory authorities. **If you intend to import this product, be aware that an import permit may be required for Customs purposes. Details of goods for which a permit is required may be found at www.tga.gov.au.**

PATIENT AND PRODUCT DETAILS - COMPLETE ALL RELEVANT SECTIONS AND PRINT CLEARLY

PATIENT DETAILS:
(initials/age or DOB, sex)

DIAGNOSIS:

MEDICINE/DEVICE:

DOSAGE/PRODUCT FORM: STRENGTH:

ROUTE/METHOD OF ADMINISTRATᴺ: DOSAGE:

DURATION OF TREATMENT:

QUANTITY TO BE SUPPLIED:

AUSTRALIAN SPONSOR OF PRODUCT:

NAME AND ADDRESS FOR SUPPLY OF PRODUCT (HOSPITAL, PHARMACIST OR DOCTOR):

MEDICAL PRACTITIONER CERTIFICATION - COMPLETE ALL SECTIONS AND PRINT CLEARLY

I, the undersigned, a registered medical practitioner in a State/Territory of Australia, certify that:

- In my opinion the patient above is a Category A patient as defined in regulation 12A of the *Therapeutic Goods Regulations 1990* /regulation 7.2 of the *Therapeutic Goods (Medical Devices) Regulations 2002* (delete as appropriate)
- I am prepared to prescribe the medicine/medical device requested; and
- I have obtained the informed consent of the patient, or the patient's legal representative, to the proposed treatment.

NAME: SIGNATURE:

PHONE: DATE   /   /

ADDRESS:

Form no. 2949 (0410)

Copyright © Rev. Dr. S. D'Montford. Monday, October 25, 2010 Mackay Qld. Australia.

Conditions of Queensland Health approval

If an approval is issued, it will contain conditions including, but not necessarily limited to the following:

1. That treatment is limited to the specified patient and in accordance with a specified treatment protocol
2. That the Amygdalin must be kept in the personal possession of the treating medical practitioner, who will, subject to 4(d) below, be responsible for destruction of any remaining stock following treatment.
3. That the treating medical practitioner explains to the patient the risks and benefits in the use of Amygdalin and obtains the patient's written consent prior to treatment.
4. **Monitoring of patient and reporting of any adverse reactions to treatment**

   (a) Prior to each episode of administration of Amygdalin after the first dose, the medical practitioner assesses the patient clinically for evidence of any adverse effects potentially arising from any previous episodes of administration of Amygdalin. Such assessment is to include monitoring the patient's temperature.

   (b) If the patient develops a fever that the medical practitioner reasonably considers may be related to the prior administration of Amygdalin, that further treatment with Amygdalin is ceased immediately and the patient's condition is investigated with microbiological cultures of appropriate clinical specimens, eg. blood.

   (c) If the patient develops any other medical condition the medical practitioner reasonably considers may be related to the prior administration of Amygdalin, that further treatment with Amygdalin is ceased immediately and the patient's condition is investigated with appropriate clinical specimens.

   (d) If the patient develops any adverse effects the medical practitioner reasonably believes are due to the administration of Amygdalin, the medical practitioner is to retain in his/her possession all remaining stocks of Amygdalin and, if requested, provide those remaining stocks to an authorised officer of Queensland Health to allow for laboratory assessment.

   (e) That the medical practitioner report in writing as soon as practicable to the Chief Executive (or delegate) of Queensland Health, any adverse effects the medical practitioner reasonably considers to have arisen from the treatment with Amygdalin. The report is to include the medical practitioner's assessment of the cause of those adverse effects and the results of any pathology or other tests undertaken to assess the patient's condition.

5. That the approval will be time limited in accordance with the specified treatment protocol.
6. That prior to consideration of any application for a re-approval after any initial approval, the approved medical practitioner will need to provide a progress treatment report, in regards to the patient's medical condition, to the Chief Executive (or delegate) of Queensland Health.

Uschi Schreiber
Director-General
Queensland Health
05 / 12 / 2006

TGA THERAPEUTIC GOODS ADMINISTRATION
PO Box 100 Woden ACT 2606 Australia
Telephone: (02)6232 8111 Facsimile: (02) 6232 8112

Health and Aged Care

Re: Approval to Import Amygdalin (Laetrile, Vitamin B17) 3gram vials

I refer to your correspondence received 12 October 2000 requesting permission to import Amygdalin (Laetrile, Vitamin B17) 3gram vials for the treatment of one of your patients under Category A of the Special Access Scheme (SAS).

Under the provisions of Regulation 5H, Item 12AA of Schedule 8 of the Customs (Prohibited Imports) Regulations, approval is hereby granted for the importation of 180 (one hundred and eighty) Amygdalin 3gram vials subject to the following conditions:

1. The Amygdalin vials are used only in accordance with your Category (A) notification dated 12/10/2000 under the SAS for the treatment of your patient LJ (DOB 8/1/1937).
2. This permit is for 180 (one hundred and eighty) vials each containing 3(three) grams Amygdalin (Laetrile, Vitamin B17) as a single consignment.
3. This permit is surrendered to Australian Customs at the time of importation.
4. All relevant State and Commonwealth laws are complied with.
5. The Commonwealth accepts no responsibility for any defects in the product related to manufacture, distribution or directions for use, including dosage or any other matter related to its use.
6. A record of distribution is kept and if requested by the Department or Australian Customs, these records must be supplied.
7. Any unused portion is appropriately disposed of in accordance with State and Commonwealth law.

This permit is valid for a period of 6 (six) months from the date of this letter.

Yours sincerely

Authorised Officer
Drug Safety and Evaluation Branch
12 October 2000

Copyright © Rev. Dr. S. D'Montford. Monday, October 25, 2010 Mackay Qld. Australia.

TAKING PERSONAL RESPONSIBILITY FOR YOUR OWN HEALTH

Remember, no matter what law any authority makes, your health is your responsibility. You have the right to make informed choices in matters concerning your own health. It is your body and you have the right to self-determination. Any authority that tells you that you do not, is turning you into a slave. You are not a slave. You have the right to disagree. You have the responsibility to yourself to choose what you believe will be the best for you. Do not give up your power. Do not give up your rights. Do not be apathetic. Do not allow yourself to be passively killed like the Eloi. Do not do nothing and allow others to determine what is right for you. Edmond Burke reminds us that: - *"Evil can only flourish where good men do nothing."* Socrates demonstrated that when you see a blatant abuse of power it is your responsibility to disobey it, so that change may occur. This precept is the corner stone of democratic civilisation.

In this matter we must question authority and demand answers to the ethical questions raised around the research, testing and possible suppression of information on B17 by those with vested interests in not finding a cancer answer.

Copyright © Rev. Dr. S. D'Montford. Monday, October 25, 2010 Mackay Qld. Australia.

REFERENCES: -

Alive & Well, One Doctor's Experience With Nutrition In The Treatment Of Cancer Patients - **Phillip Binzel**
Cancer - Why Were Still Dying To Know The Truth - **Phillip Day**
How to Get Well: Dr. Airola's Handbook of Natural Healing. **Dr. Airola Paavo**
Killing Cancer - The Jason Winters Story - **Jason Winters**
Ministry of Healing - **Ellen G. White**
Questioning Chemotherapy - **Ralph Moss**
The Cancer Industry - **Ralph Moss**
The Time Machine – **H. G. Wells**
The Unitarian Or Trophoblast Fact Of Cancer - **Ernst T. Krebs, Jr., Dr. Sc.**
World Without Cancer - **G. Edward Griffin**
The Contribution of Cytotoxic Chemotherapy to 5-year Survival in Adult Malignancies. – **G. Morgan et al.**
The Hidden Story of Cancer; **Brian Scott Peskin**
Radiation Therapy: Are We Getting Value For Money? - **M.B. Barton et al.**
http://www.b17.com.au - **Angel Rodriguez**
http://www.oasisofhope.com **The Contreras Hospital** in Mexico.
http://www.encognitive.com/node/3309
My Father **Geoffery Edward Everitt**

CHEMO ONLY 2% EFFECTIVE

Chemotherapy - 18 April 2005 - Radio National – The Health Report with Norman Swan Monday 8.pm

"Has cancer chemotherapy, the use of drugs to treat malignancies been oversold? That's the clear implication of a paper published by some Australian cancer specialists, two of whom, perhaps non-coincidentally are radiation oncologists – radio therapists. Anyway in this summary of evidence, the assertion is that chemo has only added about 2% to cancer survival. The lead author is Association Professor Graeme Morgan who's at Royal North Shore Hospital in Sydney."

References:
Morgan G et al. The Contribution of Cytotoxic Chemotherapy to 5-year Survival in Adult Malignancies. Clinical Oncology (2004);16:549-560
Barton MB et al. Radiation therapy: are we getting value for money? Clin Oncol (R Coll Radiol) 1996;8(3):206Guests on this program:
Associate Professor Graeme Morgan
Royal North Shore Hospital Sydney
Professor Michael Boyer

Copyright © Rev. Dr. S. D'Montford. Monday, October 25, 2010 Mackay Qld. Australia.

Head of Medical Oncology
Sydney Cancer Centre
Royal Prince Alfred Hospital Sydney
Further information:
Cancer - ABC Health Library A-Z
http://abc.net.au/health/library/cancer.htm

Copyright © Rev. Dr. S. D'Montford. Monday, October 25, 2010 Mackay Qld. Australia.

CANCER & LAETRILE QUOTES
http://www.whale.to/c/quotes1.html

Here is what some other prominent minds have to say about it:-

"It has been condemned as a worthless quack remedy by others because they were genuinely misinformed or because they were BAREFACED AND DELIBERATE LIARS."—Dr Richards & Frank Hourigan.

Doctors on Laetrile
After more than twenty years of such specialized work, I have found the nontoxic Nitrilosides—that is, Laetrile—far superior to any other known cancer treatment or preventative. In my opinion it is the only existing possibility for the ultimate control of cancer. *Dr. Nieper [World Without Cancer by Edward Griffin]*

So, here is a bureau of the Federal Government which, a short time before, had said that the reason Laetrile did not work was because it did not release hydrogen cyanide in the presence of cancer cells. Now, when they find that it does, they say that it is toxic. When offered an opportunity to present evidence of Laetrile's toxicity in Federal Court, they admitted that they had none. *Laetrile and the Life Saving Substance Called Cyanide by Philip Binzel, Jr., M.D.*

"I write what I see," he said repeatedly. "Laetrile is not a cure for cancer, but a good palliative drug." *REMEMBERING DR. SUGIURA by Ralph Moss*

Certainly one story that needs to be told is that of Dr. Kanematsu Sugiura. In 1975, Dr. Sugiura was, and had been for some years, one of the most respected cancer research scientists at Sloan-Kettering. In working with cancerous mice, Dr. Sugiura found that, when he used Laetrile on these mice, seventy-seven per cent of them did not develop a spread of their disease (metastatic carcinoma). He repeated this study over and over for two years. The results were always the same. Dr. Sugiura took his findings to his superiors at Sloan-Kettering, but his study was never published. Instead, Sloan-Kettering published the results of someone else who claimed that he had used Dr. Sugiura's protocol. This "someone else's" study showed that there were no beneficial effects from the use of Laetrile. Dr. Sugiura complained. He was fired. A book was written about all of this entitled The Anatomy of A Cover-up. This book has all the actual results of Dr. Sugiura's work. These results do, indeed, show the benefit of Laetrile. Dr. Sugiura stated in this book, "It is still my belief that Amygdalin cures metastases." Amygdalin is, of course, the scientific name for Laetrile. *ALIVE AND WELL by Philip E. Binzel, Jr., M.D.*

Copyright © Rev. Dr. S. D'Montford. Monday, October 25, 2010 Mackay Qld. Australia.

"The anti-cancer effect of amygdalin was demonstrated in Mexico by government sponsored reserach under Dr. Mario Soto De Leon and its use is legal. Dr Soto was the first medical director of the Cydel Clinic in Tijuana (taken over by Dr Manner) .It is very important that it be prepared and administred correctly in sufficient dosage or it will not be effective. The trial performed at the Mayo Clinic in the early 80's involved the use of the racemic mixture rather than the levo-rotary form and thus was only 10% of the strength required. In spite of this, towards the end of the experiment, the patients began to show improvement, but it was discontinued and declared ineffectual." *Dr Robert Willner, M.D.*

I ... have specialized in oncology [the study of tumors] for the past eighteen years. For the same number of years I have been using Laetrile—amygdalin in the treatment of my cancer patients. During this eighteen year period I have treated a total of over five hundred patients with Laetrile—amygdalin by various routes of administration, including the oral and the I.V. The majority of my patients receiving Laetrile—amygdalin have been in a terminal state when treatment with this material commenced. It is my carefully considered clinical judgment, as a practicing oncologist and researcher in this field, that I have obtained most significant and encouraging results with the use of Laetrile—amygdalin in the treatment of terminal cancer patients, and that these results are comparable or superior to the results I have obtained with the use of the more toxic standard cytotoxic agents. *Navarro, M.D., Manuel*

"Amygdalin (laetrile) is another key component for keeping cancer from growing and should be considered a standard, entirely safe treatment for all cancer patients." *Dr. Atkins.,M.D.*

"Laetrile is most assuredly a very potent anti-cancer factor but requires stringent methods of use in order to succeed. Amateurs invariably fail. High sounding U.S. pronouncements that 'laetrile' is toxic and ineffective are fraudulent and calculated to deceive. It will become again one of the major weapons in the cancer therapy armamentarium." *Dr Richards & Frank Hourigan.*

"You get cats in with high fevers, 105-108 degrees. There is nothing you can give them that will bring down that high a fever, except laetrile." *Dr Kearns, DVM.* (Dr Kearns uses 50mg of laetrile orally until the leukemia is under control.)

Administered to cancer patients, Laetrile has proven to be quite free from any harmful side-effects, and I would say that no anti-cancer drug could make a cancerous patient improve fAster than Laetrile. It goes without saying that Laetrile controls cancer and is quite effective wherever it is located. *Shigeaki Sakai, a prominent physician in Tokyo. [World Without Cancer by Edward Griffin]*

Copyright © Rev. Dr. S. D'Montford. Monday, October 25, 2010 Mackay Qld. Australia.

In Italy there is Professor Etore Guidetti, M.D., of the University of Turin Medical School. Dr. Guidetti spoke before the Conference of the International Union Against Cancer held in Brazil in 1954 and revealed how his use of Laetrile in terminal cancer patients had caused the destruction of a wide variety of tumors including those of the uterus, cervix, rectum, and breast. "In some cases," he said, "one has been able to observe a group of fulminating and cauliflower-like neoplastic masses resolved very rapidly" He reported that, after giving Laetrile to patients with lung cancer, he had been "able to observe, with the aid of radiography, a regression of the neoplasm or the metastases." *World Without Cancer by Edward Griffin*

The palliative action [improving the comfort and well-being of the patient] is in about 60% of the cases. Frequently, enough to be significant, I see arrest of the disease or even regression in some 15% of the very advanced cases. *Ernesto Contreras, M.D.*

"The cyano group of vitamin B-12 (cyano-cobal-amin) is more labile and potentially more harmful than the cyano group found in Laetrile. Yet we know how safe and essential vitamin B-12 is." *Dr. R.A. Passwater, testimony, FDA docket # 77N-0048.*

"When Dr. Manner reported on the total remission of breast cancer in lab animals (Using 'Laetrile in conjunction with vitamins and enzymes')..., ACS President, Ben Byrd, criticised (him) for making his announcement in public, and said such announcements should be made only in a proper scientific forum."

(Laetrile)"may be useful in sickle cell anemia...(Laetrile) used in animals with tumors show: a decrease in lung metastases; slower tumor growth; and pain relief." - *Lloyd Old, MD, vice president, Sloan-Kettering Institute for Cancer Research, at FDA 7-2-1974.*

As an explosive internal issue, the laetrile affair has almost attained the order of magnitude of the Vietnam conflict. I still do not see how some of the exponents of official American cancer medicine, and certain bureaucracies in Washington, are going to emerge from this affair with clean hands. The effect of this bitter almond substance is not strong, and can be observed only if the defense mechanisms are in operation. In any event, it can and was clearly proven both clinically and experimentally, with positive results, at both the famous Sloan-Kettering Institute in New York, and at the Pasteur Institute in Paris. An enormous suppression story was leaked to the press by a member of the New York institute. A rather mysterious "testing" in five clinics, including the famous Mayo Clinic, led to the strong suspicion that certain oral (not intravenous) doses of laetrile were tested after having been previously and intentionally "contaminated" at the National Cancer Institute in Washington, with a certain highly poisonous cyano urea combination. Officially, a "purification" was admitted. *Dr. Hans A. Nieper of Germany has this to say about B–17*

Medical Fascism
By 1978, 70,000 US cancer patients had taken Laetrile for cancer treatment, and many of those had gone to Tijuana to receive it. The turning point for the clinics came with passage of the North American Free Trade Agreement (NAFTA), which facilitated greater cooperation among the antifraud authorities of Canada, the United States, and Mexico. In 1994, the tripartite members of NAFTA formed the Mexico-United States-Canada Health Fraud Work Group, or MUCH, whose brief is to strengthen the 3 countries' ability to prevent cross-border health fraud. Under the auspices of MUCH and its members, regulatory crackdowns began in earnest early in 2001. *Tijuana Cancer Clinics in the Post-NAFTA Era by Ralph W. Moss, PhD*

(In)"1970, the Pennsylvania Health Dept., swooped down on a meeting...after the movie Laetrile,...was shown. The film was confiscated and the association president arrested." *Vitamin B-17--Forbidden Weapon against Cancer: The Fight for Laetrile by Culbert, Michael L.*

"...In July 1974 About 15 agents (of Cal. Food and Drug) arrested me on the charge of selling Laetrile and other substances in the diagnosis, cure and alleviation of cancer. In Citrus Municipal Court, West Covina, on Feb 3, 1975, Judge Sam Cianchetti declared this statute unconstitutional. On Oct. 1974, I received a phone call from ...police at 1 (AM, Saturday morning) and he told me that my office was broken into. I went down to my office ...and 2 agents arrest(ed) me on a felony charge - conspiracy ...The law states that before you are even arrested, they must give you a hearing (Cal. Health Code 1707.4) (Another) judge denied this motion for a ...hearing and he gave no reason." *Dr. James Privitera; Roswell Park Memorial Institute,; Scripps Clinic; "The Nutritional Battle."*

"...there is no basis for the use of Laetrile in man based on data derived from experiments on animals.": - Dr. Jesse Steinfeld, Surgeon General, US Public Health Service.

"Dr. (Howard H.)Beard 'was ...charged with...mail fraud...rendering fake and medically worthless cancer reports...Postal Investigators satisfied themselves the reports were willfully falsified...' On Oct. 30, 1967, Dr. Beard was sentenced in US Federal Court, Ft. Worth, Texas, 'to...mail fraud...He alleged he could detect the presence of cancer in urine in 95% of all tests made." - FDA Papers, 1967-1968 (in ACS, Unproven Methods of Cancer Management, 1967).

Copyright © Rev. Dr. S. D'Montford. Monday, October 25, 2010 Mackay Qld. Australia.

"Not that there are not real quacks in the field of cancer... But ...no legitimate MD...with a thriving practice and after years of study and faithful service would give all that up to become a quack and subject himself and his family to Hell..." - John Richardson, MD, Laetrile Case Histories.

"Federal, state, and local police raided Dr. (John) Richardson's Clinic,...beat up a(n) aide, manhandled a nurse, and dragged the business manager off in handcuffs."

"Important Elements of FDA Policy: Encourage local medical licensing authorities to investigate and take appropriate action to deal with the use of Laetrile by physicians in their practice." - FDA Division of Federal-State Relations Director, 1974.

"The data provided by the McNaughton Foundation certainly indicates some activity (of Laetrile) in animal tumor systems.: - Dr. Carl Baker, Director, NCI 1970-1972.

"The Food, Drug, and Cosmetic ACT,...defines any article 'intended for use in the diagnosis, ...treatment, or prevention of disease' as a 'drug'...Water...to an individual dying of thirst could ...be called a 'drug." - Michael Culbert, Freedom From Cancer.

"..The woman...had been relieved of her cancer by Laetrile.....In the hospital they would not inject Laetrile as it was illegal. She died. This so incensed the editors of the Santa Ana Register (Dean and Martinez) that they wrote ("Laetrile Story") a series of articles on cancer and the true story for the first time was sent by UPI to (almost) every country in the world."   - Howard H. Beard, ScD, PhD, Yale U. The Anthrone Test.

"Dr. (Donald R.) Cole (formerly of Sloan-Kettering and St. Vincent's Hospital in New York) was charged with three counts: giving false hope to the terminally ill, using experimental drugs illegally, and practicing medicine in an unlawful and dishonest manner....The illegal drug charge was defined as the use of vitamins, enzymes, and Laetrile. ...Dr. Cole administered Laetrile at the request of patients in the legally prescribed manner with a signed affidavit....An oncologist from Rosewell Park (Memorial Institute) who was brought in by the hearing panel...could not substantiate a single case of incompetence or negligence. ...Dr. Cole's license was revoked." - CCS, Cancer Control Journal, January 1978.

"...The ...experts of the FDA have declared Laetrile to be worthless...quackery and fraud...These experts are the professional descendants of experts...confident that mental illness should be cured by drilling holes in the skull, the better to let the demons out. ...This is the

Orwellian fashion in which the medical establishment throws its weight around...." - James Kilpatrick, Washington Star, 1976.

(In)" 1970, in Camp Hill, Pennsylvania....Bruce Butt...convened a meeting at which he showed...Nature's Answer to Cancer. The film was made by the International Association of Cancer Victims and Friends (IACVF)....(The) attorney...defending Mr. Butt (said): Mr. Butt is criminally charged with 'unlawfully procuring and showing the film, Nature's Answer to Cancer, which the state of Pennsylvania claims 'constitutes dissemination of false or misleading advertisement, concerning the efficacy of Laetrile , as a cure or treatment for cancer'. (And) this constitutes a misbranding of a drug, ...although ...all parties ("stipulate") that no drug ("Laetrile") was sold or offered for sale! Present at the preliminary hearing were...USDHEW, and the FTC,...and FDA... Again when the film was advertised for showing in a public theater in San Jose, the owner was threatened by the DA's office with a criminal charge, arrest, and seizure of the film." - IACVF, Cancer News Journal, 1964.

"...Medical mankind in particular, were supposed to be waiting for the advent of some new scientific discovery concerning the nature of cancer... ...The physical martyrdom was lacking; but there are, as I can testify from experience, many more ways than one of burning a scientific man at the stake." - John Beard. D.Sc., The Enzyme Treatment of Cancer and its Scientific Basis. c. 1911 AD.

"Dr. Helen Calvin ...spearheaded ...Indiana to approve Laetrile, and then she used the Laetrile and metabolic program ...until the FDA arbitrarily and illegally held up her Laetrile shipments ...patients started dying ...When four of them had died, Dr. Calvin ended her own life." - Arlin Brown, Cancer Victory Bulletin, Oct. 1978.

"Dr. Emory Thurston, PhD, ScD, (lecturer, College of Pharmacy, USC; member APA (American Pharmaceutical Assoc.), Executive Secretary of Nutritional Research (had) ...inspectors from the Calif. Food and Drug office armed with a search warrant, (who) raided his business office. They confiscated several bottles of Laetrile...and every piece of literature that contained the word 'cancer'. (They) serve(d) a warrant for the arrest of Dr. Thurston on the charge of selling Laetrile and practicing medicine without a license. He was taken to county jail..." International Association of Cancer Friends and Victims, Cancer News Journal, 1973.

(MD) "Certificate...of John A. Richardson...is revoked." - California Board of Medical Quality Assurance, 1975.

Copyright © Rev. Dr. S. D'Montford. Monday, October 25, 2010 Mackay Qld. Australia.

"..Dr. Krebs...is facing the possibility of a jail sentence stemming from violation of a 1977 court order not to speak publicly about Laetrile" - Voice of Medical Freedom, April 1981.

"Dr. Ernest J. Krebs, Jr., (and his secretary) ...began serving a six-month prison term in May (1983) in the San Francisco County Jail. (They) were found guilty of continuing to promote the merits of Laetrile in cancer therapy in violation of terms of probation they had originally secured following their 1973 conviction." - Choice, spring 1983.

"In 1977, when the Laetrile bill was first introduced to the North Dakota Legislature, I was the only MD to testify for it...After that, my successful tenure...was ended and I was called before the State Medical Examiners Board in ND, for using vitamins and Laetrile. ...I travelled...to work...with Dr. Davis, Dr. Cole, and Dr. Manner...When I returned...I was refused re-instatement to the medical staff...We are being investigated by the (state) attorney general's office because our methods are not 'usual and customary'."

"After presenting a rather effective lecture on cancer...the windshield was shot out of my car on the road back to San Francisco. The next night the glass window in the tail gate was shot out (300 miles removed from the first shooting). The police said, 'maybe someone is trying to tell you something'. The late Arthur Harris, M.D. was threatened by two men with assassination if he continued to use laetrile. Since that time we have de-centralised the work so that, if any two of us are shot out of the saddle, it will have only a slight negative effect on the program."---Dr. Krebs

"...testifying for Dr. Privitera...To these 19 cancer victims, the enforcement of (California) Health and Safety Code Sect. 1701.1, the denial of them medical treatment, albeit unorthodox, albeit unapproved by a state agency, must surely take on a Kafka-esque, a nightmare quality. No demonstrated public anger, no compelling interest of the state warrants an Orwellian intrusion into the most private of zones of privacy." - California Supreme Court Chief Justice, Rose Bird, dissenting opinion.

"In 1964 (we) conduct(ed) an intensive investigation of Laetrile...conclud(ing) that there was no justification for making (it) illegal...Yet, 16 years after... , doctors are still being jailed for (it). Dr. James Privitera;,... was recently released from 55 days...much of it doing hard labor...on a road gang...If he were solely interested in making money, as he points out, there is a great deal more to be made from traditional cancer treatments, than by use of Laetrile." - Santa Ana, The Register, April 13, 1980.

"I had to stand three expensive trials in California courts, where in all three actions against me, the charges were dismissed. Then I had to stand an

Copyright © Rev. Dr. S. D'Montford. Monday, October 25, 2010 Mackay Qld. Australia.

even longer and more expensive trial in Federal Court in San Diego, where I was convicted of 'conspiring to smuggle Laetrile' and was fined $30,000. ... Cal. then revoked my license." - John Richardson, MD.

Fraud
"The (Laetrile) efficacy tests...clinically in humans..(by) the US NCI...were obviously conducted so that a negative result could be formulated. The limited number and types of human cancer cases selected...the omission of necessary additional measures ('e.g dietary'), the far too short observation periods, and the undefined chemical properties of the (Laetrile)... all contributed to devaluation of...conclusions."
"... The cancer statutes (are) discriminatory against the cancer patient.... No other disease is so restricted by politics.... It is also discriminatory against the Negro because Laetrile helps sickle cell anemia.... It is discriminatory against the poor because the poor can't afford to go to Mexico or Germany (for therapies outlawed in the US)..."
"The Food, Drug, and Cosmetic ACT,...defines any article 'intended for use in the diagnosis, ...treatment, or prevention of disease' as a 'drug'...Water...to an individual dying of thirst could ...be called a 'drug." - Michael Culbert, Freedom From Cancer.

"The (MSKCC) Memorial Sloan-Kettering Cancer Center report on amygdalin, or Laetrile(:) It is incomplete because at least half a dozen experiments with amygdalin performed at the (MSKCC) between 1972 and 1976 have been omitted from the report. (These,) the positive experiments (showing effectivity against cancer) with amygdalin, carried out by veteran researcher Kanematsu Sugiura appear to be valid and are not successfully challenged by the report. (In contrast,) there are numerous errors in many of these (reported) experiments which allegedly prove amygdalin's ineffectiveness as a palliative or cure for cancer." - Second Opinion, Special Report: Laetrile at Sloan Kettering, 1977, published January 1978.

According to Richard Walters, Dr. James Cason of the University of California, Berkeley, analyzed the compound used in the Mayo Clinic study using infrared spectrophotometry and determined that it did not contain amygdalin at all.

The California Medical Association (CMA) evaluated the records of some 44 patients who received Laetrile therapy for cancer at a number of California hospitals. The review was irrefutably slapdash (Krebs had refused to cooperate with the CMA in a more controlled study since the CMA would not agree to let a Laetrile friend direct the study), inasmuch as these records, never intended for a study of any kind, were deficient in numerous respects. Patients were widely diverse, were treated with various therapies, including Laetrile, and the extent or even the reality of their disease poorly defined in many cases. They were given, by today's standards, nearly negligible doses

Copyright © Rev. Dr. S. D'Montford. Monday, October 25, 2010 Mackay Qld. Australia.

of Laetrile. (In each case, Dr. Burk says, less Laetrile was given during the entire course of treatment than is given in a single injection today.) Yet the conclusion of the CMA, circulated without supporting data, was that Laetrile had now been thoroughly tested and that "no satisfactory evidence has been produced to indicate any significant cytotoxic effect of Laetrile on the cancer cell."

The authors of these conclusions state also that some six pathologists who examined tissues of Laetrile-treated patients were of the "unanimous opinion" that "in no instance could any recognizable effect of a chemotherapeutic agent be observed in the histology of these various neoplasms." This was a witting lie, for when the raw data was, perhaps unwittingly, affixed to a reissue of the report in 1963 there was evidence that some of these pathologists had reported on a number of possible, amygdalin-related chemotherapeutic effects, e.g. "...hemorrhagic necrosis of tumor is extensive....an interpretation of chemotherapeutic effect might be entertained...." (This evidence may be found in Appendix Three of "Report by Cancer Advisory Council on Treatment of Cancer with Beta-Cyanogenic Glucosides ['Laetrile'].") Laetrile: The Goddamned-Contraband-Apricot Connection. It may not be the "magic bullet" but it scares the hell out of the American Cancer Society by David M. Rorvik

"My analyses and conclusions differ diametrically from those of the Southern Research Institute/National Cancer Institute report wherein it is concluded that amygdalin 'does not possess activity in the Lewis lung carcinoma system.'.... My analysis of the data is that it is overwhelmingly positive." — Dean Burk, while serving as Chief of the Cytochemistry Division of the National Cancer Institute, March 22, 1974, letter to Dr. Seymour Perry, Deputy Director, NCI Division of Cancer Treatment.

A control for cancer is known, and it comes from nature. But it is not widely available to the public, because it cannot be patented, and therefore is not commercially attractive to the pharmaceutical industry.

Here's what happened. They began a series of tests on Laetrile and they turned it over to their top laboratory technician Dr. Kanematsu Sugiura, a Japanese fellow, he was sort of at the end of his career. He was very well known, held at high esteem by all of his associates. He was mr laboratory test. Whatever Sugiura said, went, for everybody, so they gave it to Sugiura. Sugiura ran his tests and this was his report. He came to five conclusions. Fist of all, he said, it improved the general health of the mice that he was using. Secondly it appeared to relieve their pain. Thirdly it inhibited the growth of tumors. Fourth it stopped the spread of tumors.. and five it acted as a cancer prevention. That was his official finding. And at the end of this report, this is a quote ' Dr has never observed complete regression of these tumors in all his cosmic experience with other chemotherapeutic agents' end quote.

Copyright © Rev. Dr. S. D'Montford. Monday, October 25, 2010 Mackay Qld. Australia.

Congressman John Kelsey used the Freedom of Information Act to obtain a copy of the minutes of the board of directors of Sloan Kettering dated July 2nd 1974. And from the minutes it said quote 'Sloan Kettering is not enthusiastic about studying Amygdalin, but would like to study cyanide releasing drugs.' end quote. Now if you understand that sentence you understand everything that I'm talking to you about today.

Rockefeller had become very influential in the pharmaceutical industry first in the United States and now around the world, but has chosen to remain pretty much behind the scenes. They know that it wouldn't look good to have the Rockefeller name popping up under all branches of industry. It's bad enough, they feel, that they're so well identified with the oil industry. How much worse it would be if they were also identified as being a dominant factor pharmaceutical industry.

Almost over night all of the major universities, which we now consider to be major universities in the field of medicine, received large grants from these sources and also accepted 1, 2, or 3 of these people that I mentioned on their board of directors, and the schools literally were taken over by the financial interests that put up the money. The Science and Politics of Cancer A discourse by G. Edward Griffin

"The oral (Laetrile) had been 'toxified' by adding cyano-urea in the NCI... (NCI's) Mayo (Clinic) dismissed well responding patients to discard them from statistical evaluation...This kind of fraud which I expressed...and which was openly published...has...not resulted in any denial." - Hans Nieper, MD, President, International Academy of Preventive Medicine; Director, German Society for Medical Tumor Treatment; author of over 200 articles, listed in Who's Who of World Science, and many other credentials.

"The slight variations in extracting procedure cause many of the amygdalin (Vitamin B-17, Laetrile) molecules to change to a form unknown to nature(:) isomers...There are ...purveyors who label their 'iso-amygdalin' products 'amygdalin' contrary to all of the recognized specs...For commercial or political purposes, they certainly cannot justify such a fallacy...This scientific heresy and commercial fraud...(is) tremendously reducing the effectiveness of amygdalin therapy. ...To mislabel iso-amygdalin as amygdalin is scientifically, medically, and morally indefensible." - Dr. Ernst T. Krebs, Jr. discoverer of vitamins B-15 and B-17.

Suppression Conspiracy
"When results of the (Laetrile) toxicity tests at Loyola (University, Chicago) were complete, (Dr. Harold Manner, Chairman Biology Dept., author 50 articles, 5 texts) asked NCI to publish the findings in Journal NCI. This the agency refused to do. Publication in other journals was also denied him." - National Health Federation, Bulletin, Nov. 1977.

Copyright © Rev. Dr. S. D'Montford. Monday, October 25, 2010 Mackay Qld. Australia.

"I and many other Members of Congress have received a large volume of mail from individuals...benefited from Laetrile treatments,...who believe the Government is party to a conspiracy to suppress an inexpensive, non-toxic and effective anti-cancer drug. ...public confidence in our Government has not been strengthened by the highly unusual actions of the FDA in first advising...that clinical studies with Laetrile could be initiated and then terminating this authorization..."

(There is a) "deeply held conviction of a large number of Americans that they are being forced by their Government to leave the country in order to obtain therapy with a drug that is both safe and effective for the control of cancer... (A) review should be done by cancer experts who have no conflicting interest and who are able to evaluate the evidence objectively...In light of the tremendous sums of money that have been spent with relatively little productivity..., I find it very surprising that the NCI has not sought on its own initiative to do further animal testing with this drug which apparently has shown some activity in the tests sponsored by the McNaughton Foundation." - US Congressman L.H. Fountain (in a letter to HEW Secretary), 1971.

"The ...Times ...headlined the Assistant US Attorney ...grand jury investigation of myself, six months before the grand jury was even selected. ...Soon after Bantam printed 200,000 copies of our book, ...Times bought the serial rights to it. ...After sitting on the serial rights for a suitable period, the ...Times ...unctuously begged Bantam to be released from their gentlemen's agreement, and the serial market had been destroyed. ...Most libraries will not accept a book that has not been reviewed by the ...Times or its affiliate..." - John Richardson, MD, Richardson Newsletter, 1979.

"A nationwide Harris Poll showed that the public favoured the use of Laetrile by a 30% margin. ...In over 250 cases of cancer with which I have been associated, all of whom used (Laetrile, vitamin) B-17, not a single one had side effects as a result...." - Leon Chaitow, ND, DO, Member, British Naturopathic and Osteopathic Association., An End to Cancer?

"Every study to date has not found any evidence of efficacy of Laetrile, and if there was one shred of evidence from animal or cell systems, I would issue an IND." — Dr. Alexander Schmidt, Commissioner of the Food and Drug Administration.

"20 Federal agents in 13 undercover cars...arrested and...jailed...Robert Bradford (President, Committee for Freedom of Choice in Cancer Therapy.)...on leave from Stanford University...and two Mexicans..on charges of conspiracy to smuggle (Laetrile)."

"Why is it that the US Supreme Court says physicians may perform abortions on the ground that the physician - patient relationship is inviolable; but that the same physician is not permitted to prescribe Laetrile for his

Copyright © Rev. Dr. S. D'Montford. Monday, October 25, 2010 Mackay Qld. Australia.

patients...but not to destroy life but to save it? Why are we told that a patient has the "right to die with dignity", but may not take Laetrile in an attempt to live?" - Alan Stang, American Opinion (from Princeton paper, "The Political Implications of Laetrile...").

"In a study of 252 people who attended a Laetrile symposium sponsored by the CCS (Cancer Control Society), we found that those attending were predominantly white, female, rural, and highly educated." - Gerald E. Markle and James C. Petersen, Professors of Sociology, Western Michigan University; editors of Politics, Science, and Cancer; the Laetrile Phenomenon.

(Maurice Kowan, MD) "served three months in jail, paid a fine of $3,000, and was forbidden to see a cancer patient...for three years. Before sentencing, it had been suggested to Dr. Kowan...to sign a statement that...Laetrile...had proved no benefit....He refused any 'deals'..." - Betty Lee Morales, "The National Health Federation, Do We Need It?".

"The jury had never been allowed to see any evidence that Laetrile actually worked. (Yes Virginia, they can bury medical breakthroughs in court this way also.) Dr. Kowan...was...age 70..." - G.E. Griffin, Cancer Control Journal, 1977.

"...In treating approximately 100 cancer cases, most ...terminal, (Dr. Kowan) was able to achieve dramatic relief from pain in virtually every single case. ...Several patients told...that the fees Dr. Kowan charged were ridiculously low.... Dr. Kowan was sentenced (including) 30 days in the workhouse..." - David Martin, Staff member, US Senate Internal Security Committee, in Cancer News Journal, Jan 1971.

"In truth, as time has gone on, I have found much evidence to make me believe that the FDA had, indeed, done a great many studies on Laetrile. The problem was they apparently had found that — when properly used with other vitamins, minerals, enzymes and diet — Laetrile could be very beneficial to many cancer patients. There was no way the FDA was going to admit this! For more than fifteen years they had been saying that Laetrile was of no value. To come out now and say that they had been wrong was unthinkable. The fuss and furor that would have come from the people of this country would have been tremendous. Congress, rapidly, would have been forced to do away with the FDA. To the government, this would have been a terrible loss. After all, the "most important" function of any government bureaucracy is to perpetuate itself. It is my opinion, and only an opinion, that it was easier for the FDA to say that they had done no studies than to reveal what their studies had actually shown. It was far less dangerous to go through Administrative Hearings than to admit that they were wrong."---- ALIVE AND WELL by Philip E. Binzel, Jr., M.D.

Basically the attitude was best expressed by Lewis Thomas, the president of the centre, who told my boss, as he would not see me, "I am not going to die on the barricades for Laetrile. It is not a cure, it is only a palliative, (meaning it relieves pain and stops the spread of cancer), if it were a cure it might be a different story, but I am not going to give up my career, to die on the barricades". That's how they justified it in their own minds. I could not do that, nor could Dr Sugiura, who never renounced the results of his own studies, despite the fact they put enormous pressure on him to do so.

If you look at the board of directors of MSK you will find that the drug industry has a dominant position on that board. One company in particular, Bristol Myers, which produces between 40 -50% of all the chemotherapy in the world, and they have top positions at MSK hospital. They are selling their own drugs to that particular hospital but they have written into the by-laws of the centre that it does not constitute a conflict of interest to sell their company drugs to the centre. They get around it by not taking a salary. They are not paid, they are volunteers. Look what happens. You have a man like Benno Schmidt, who was first head of the president's cancer panel under Nixon, then becomes head of MSK. He then goes on using the knowledge he gained at MSK to set up his own drug company to make tens of millions of dollars......The chairman of the board of Bristol Myers, the main company producing anti-cancer drugs, who also happens to be on the board of MSK, is also on the board of the New York Times. Everybody's brother in law is an oncologist, or on the board of somebody else's something or other, so it is a money making thing for the establishment. A hundred and seven billion, with a B, dollars a year business, and we are not going to get rid of it easily. Interview of Dr Ralph Moss, Ph.D.

The Network of Evil
"Such letters...from the FDA, are, filled with objectively demonstrable lies, practiced deceptions and deviousness, red herrings, directed misinformation, misdirected information, etc. ...Once FDA-NCI-AMA-ACS...concedes that Laetrile anti-tumor efficacy was indeed even once observed...a permanent crack in bureaucratic armor has taken place." - Dr. Dean Burke, co-founder, National Cancer Institute (NCI), Cyto-chemistry section: open letter July 3, 1973.

"Available scientific evidence does not support claims that Laetrile is effective in treating cancer or any other disease. ...The consensus of available scientific evidence does not support claims that Laetrile is an effective anti-cancer treatment, either in animal studies or in human clinical trials. Cancer cells do not seem to be more susceptible to the effects of Laetrile than normal cells. The successes claimed by its supporters are based on individual (anecdotal) reports, testimonials, and publicity issued by promoters. "--ACS [2008]

Copyright © Rev. Dr. S. D'Montford. Monday, October 25, 2010 Mackay Qld. Australia.

"Laetrile: Laetrile is one of the best known alternative cancer treatments. Proponents of Laetrile claim it selectively destroys cancer cells and relieves pain, although three clinical trials, as well as studies supported by the National Cancer Institute, have found it to be ineffective in the cure, improvement, or stabilization of cancer."---American Cancer Society (ACS) 1998 http://www.cancer.org/frames.html

"On the very day that the NCI announced Laetrile's alleged worthlessness..., West Virginia became the 24th state to allow the use of Laetrile...In signing the bill into law, Gov. Jay Rockefeller said the study, 'made no difference at all.' - National Health Federation, July, 1981.

"It is not true that the Mafia play any part in the battle for the free and unhampered use of Laetrile...if they had it is most probable that Laetrile would have been cleared by the FDA years ago." — Andrew McNaughton, Chairman of the McNaughton Foundation.

"Does it make sense that a (Laetrile) smuggler who is supposed (by the Medical Establishment - Ed.) to be making millions of dollars off of what he is smuggling, would spend five years of his life trying to legalize it.?" - Frank Salaman, grad., northwestern U.

Copyright © Rev. Dr. S. D'Montford. Monday, October 25, 2010 Mackay Qld. Australia. - Word count 10,723

PERSONAL NOTES

www.ingramcontent.com/pod-product-compliance
Lightning Source LLC
Chambersburg PA
CBHW050608300426
44112CB00013B/2131